MINDFUL MATH

Use Your **STATISTICS** to Solve these Puzzling Pictures

Blackline masters by Ann McNair

Illustrations by Robyn Djuritschek

PUBLISHER'S NOTE

Tarquin were delighted when Ann and Robyn approached us with the idea for the three books in this series. We have published and sold hundreds of thousands of copies of similar books for younger ages – see below – and had great success with other entertaining approaches to homework, revision and reinforcement. Books such as Mini Mathematical Murder Mysteries, Mathematical Team Games, Mathematical Treasure Hunts and Mathstraks activities – make up a wonderful set of resources for every style of learning and teaching.

The three Mindful Math titles join these books in our Tarquin eReader system, which allows you to add ebooks and then search for what you want so that you can print activities. We heavily discount ebook access for those who buy hard copy books, so they are as easy to use as possible.

See our full range at www.tarquingroup.com, sign up for our newsletters and follow us on Twitter and Facebook @tarquingroup for news, offers and new resources. All our books are available in the USA and Canada through www.ipgbook.com.

OTHER COLORING BOOKS FROM TARQUIN

Mindful Math – Algebra   ISBN 9781913565770
Mindful Math – Geometry   ISBN 9781913565787

For more coloring books for secondary ages, see the **By Design** series on our website

FOR AGES 5-11

Arithmetic Arithmetic   ISBN 9781899618149
The Multiplication Tables Colouring Book   ISBN 9780906212851
The Second Multiplication Tables Colouring Book   ISBN 9781899618309

© 2021 Ann McNair and Robyn Djuritschek

Published by Tarquin Publications
Suite 74, 17 Holywell Hill
St Albans AL1 1DT, UK

www.tarquingroup.com

Distributed by IPG Books,
814 N. Franklin St.,
Chicago, IL 60610, USA

www.ipgbook.com

Design: Karl Hunt

Printed in the USA

ISBN (Book)   9781913565794
ISBN (EBook) 9781913565824

CONTENTS

INTERPRETING DIAGRAMS

PART 1: The pictogram shows the number of complaints received by a delivery company in one week.

1. How many complaints were received on Wednesday?
2. How many complaints were received on Monday?
3. On Friday there were 12 complaints. How many squares are needed?
4. What is the total number of complaints in this week?
5. The following week the complaints are reduced by one third. How many complaints did they receive?

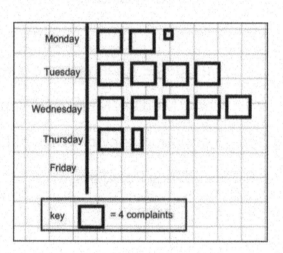

PART 2: The bar chart shows the shoes sizes of a class of students.

6. How many students take size 7?
7. How many students take a shoe size of a 6 at most?
8. How many students are in the class?
9. What percentage of the class take a size greater than a 6?
10. 5 new students are added to the class. Their shoes sizes are 6, 6, 7, 7.5 and 8. What is the new percentage of the class that take greater than a size 6?

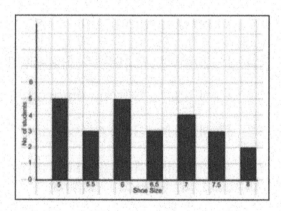

PART 3: A group of students recorded the number of vehicles in the parking area at school.

11. What was the most number of vehicles in the parking area?

12. How many vehicles were already in the parking area when they started counting?

13. How many vehicles were in the parking area at 5pm?

14. How many more vehicles were in the parking area at 3pm than at 7pm?

15. Estimate how many vehicles there were at 10am.

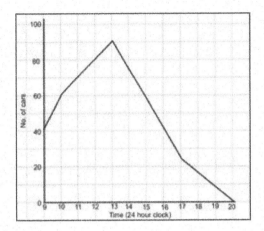

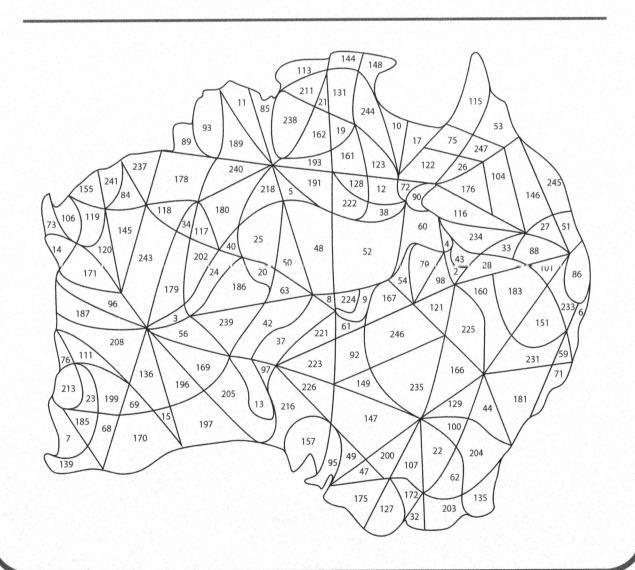

2

AVERAGES 1

(mode, median, mean from a list)

PART 1: Write down the mode for each set of numbers.

1. 6, 7, 7, 9, 12, 15
2. 14, 19, 24, 17, 11, 17, 14, 17
3. 45, 46, 54, 45, 43, 56, 60
4. 1, 2, 1, 1, 2, 1, 2, 1, 1, 2, 2
5.

Number of cars	Frequency
0	3
1	7
2	6
3	10
4	12
5	3

PART 2: Work out the median.

6. 62, 65, 69, 70, 72, 76, 77
7. 26, 21, 27, 24, 24, 22, 28
8. 13, 15, 16, 20, 12, 10
9. 7, 32, 19, 46, 53, 12, 4, 27
10. For the table in Part 1, question 5.

PART 3: Work out the mean.

11. 6, 23, 16, 8, 7
12. 37, 24, 25, 33, 40, 27
13. 100, 124, 82, 91, 73
14. The mean of the numbers 1-11 inclusive.
15. The mean of the first 10 even numbers.

AVERAGES 2

(mean from a frequency table)

PART 1: The number of candies in a packet is recorded in the table.

1. How many packets have 23 candies in them?
2. What is the mode number of candies?
3. How many packets were counted?
4. What is the total number of candies?
5. Calculate the mean number of candies per packet (to the nearest whole number).

No. of candies	Frequency
20	1
21	1
22	7
23	6
24	5

PART 2: The table shows the waiting time for a ride, in minutes.

6. How many people waited between 5 and 10 minutes?
7. What is the frequency of the modal time?
8. How many people waited for the ride?
9. What is the value of the total of mid-point × frequency?
10. Estimate the value of the mean time?

Time	Frequency
$0 \leq t < 5$	12
$5 \leq t < 10$	17
$10 \leq t < 15$	16
$15 \leq t < 20$	25
$20 \leq t < 25$	4
$25 \leq t < 30$	6

PART 3: Adam plays 50 games in an arcade. He can win tickets on each game. The table shows the frequency of the number of tickets won.

11. Work out the missing frequency.
12. What is the total number of tickets won?
13. What is the mean number of tickets per game?

No. of tickets	Frequency
0	4
1	4
2	
3	6
4	10
5	6
6	10
7	2
8	3

14. Adam wants to exchange his tickets for a gift that is 500 tickets. How many more tickets does he need?

15. Estimate how many more games Adam needs to play to get the tickets he needs.

MEAN, MEDIAN, MODE AND RANGE

PART 1:

1. Calculate the range of the numbers 6, 7, 10, 8, 8, 9.
2. Calculate the range of the numbers 6.2, 7.3, 8.8, 1.5, 4.1.
3. Calculate the range of the numbers 7, 9, −2, 13, 9, 8, 19, −8, 1.
4. Five numbers have a range of 14. Four of the numbers are 20, 22, 31 and 25. What is the smallest possible value of the fifth number?
5. For question 4, what is the largest possible value of the fifth number?

PART 2: Seven students take a general knowledge test to try to make it into the school quiz team. The test is out of 40.

Their scores are: 31, 26, 23, 35, 32, 38, 35.

6. What is the mode score?
7. What is the median score?
8. What is the mean score?
9. What is the range of the scores?
10. To get into the quiz team you need to score 75% or more. How many students make the team?

PART 3: 8 boys and 6 girls from a class skip 100m. The times, to the nearest second for the girls are: 15, 20, 24, 18, 20, and 23. The boy's mean time is 25 seconds and their range is 14 seconds.

11. What is the range of the girl's times?
12. What is the mean of the girl's times?
13. What is the total of the boy's times?
14. The quickest boy took 14 seconds. What was the time of the slowest boy?
15. What is the overall mean of all the children?

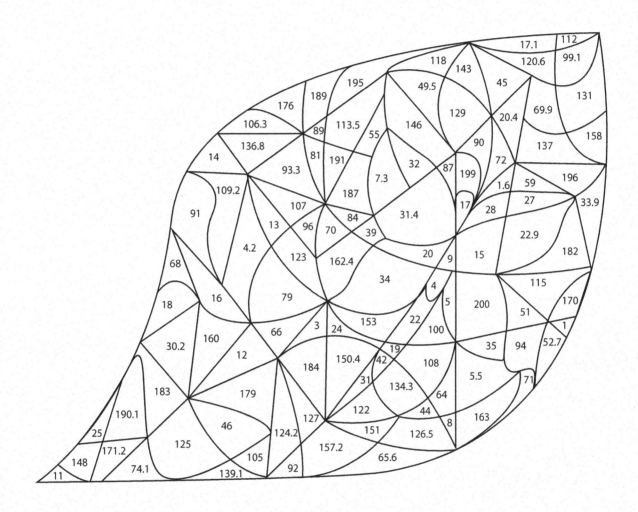

CORRELATION

(including line of best fit)

PART 1: The scattergraph shows the age of a puppy versus weight.

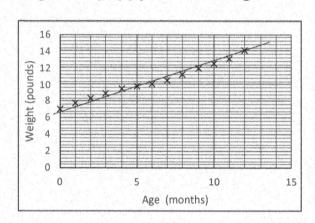

1. What is the weight of the puppy at 6 months?
2. At what age is the puppy 13 pounds?
3. What is the birth weight of the puppy?
4. How much weight did the puppy gain in the first 9 months?
5. Use the line of best fit to estimate the age at 12 pounds.

PART 2: The scattergraph shows the scores students achieved in math and science tests.

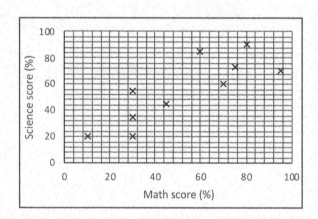

6. What was the lowest science score?
7. What was the highest math score?
8. One student got 60 in the science test. What was his score in the math test?
9. Which subject results gave the largest range? Shade in the range.
10. What is the score of the student that achieved the same score in both tests?

PART 3: The scattergraph shows the distance from the center of Edinburgh, Scotland against rent per month for a flat.

11. How much does it cost to live 10km from the center?

12. What is the cheapest rent?

13. Julie has £1100 to spend on rent. How close to the center can she live?

14. How much is the monthly rent for the center of Edinburgh.

15. Estimate the cost of living 25km from the center.

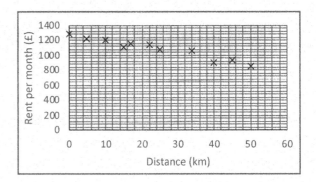

6
FREQUENCY POLYGONS

PART 1: The frequency polygon show how many times people went to the movies in a month.

1. How many people went 3 times?
2. What was the most popular number of times?
3. How many people never went?
4. How many people were surveyed in total?
5. What is the mean number of times visited (to 1 dp)?

PART 2: The frequency polygon shows the number of pets owned by a class of children.

6, 7, 8. Complete the table
9. What is the modal number of pets owned?
10. Calculate the mean number of pets owned (to 1 dp).

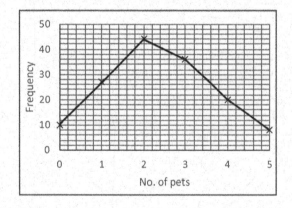

No. of pets	Frequency
0	
1	27
2	
3	
4	20
5	8

PART 3: The frequency polygon shows the time spent in minutes in a department store.

11, 12, 13, 14. Complete the table
15. Calculate an estimate for the mean time spent in the store (to the nearest whole number).

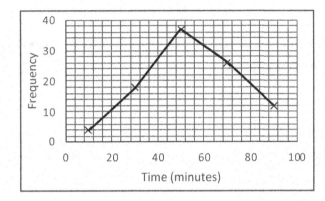

No. of pets	Frequency
$0 \leq t < 20$	4
$20 \leq t < 40$	
$40 \leq t < \_$	37
$60 \leq t < 80$	
$80 \leq t < 100$	12
TOTAL	

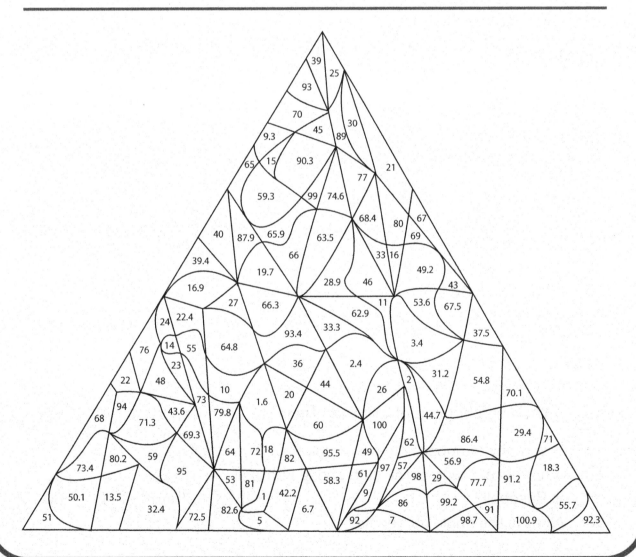

PIE CHARTS

PART 1: Mr Cochrane is preparing data for a pie chart. He is looking at the grades for last year's History test.

1. How many people took the History test?
2. How many degrees would represent 1 student?
3. Calculate the angle for grade A+
4. Calculate the angle for grade C
5. Calculate the angle for grade D

CHALLENGE: Draw the pie chart for the data.

Grade	Frequency
A+	4
A	7
B	12
C	8
D	3
E	2

PART 2: Maria has surveyed 45 students to find out their favourite color. She has drawn an accurate pie chart of her results.

6. What is the value of the angle for blue?
7. How many people said yellow?
8. How many people said blue?
9. How many people said green?
10. What percentage did not choose blue?

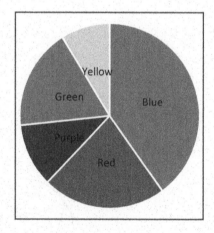

PART 3: A youth club is looking to offer more sports activities to its members. The table shows the preferences of the members.

11. How many members does the club have?
12. What percentage of the club chose Football or Baseball?
13. What is the angle for tennis?

Sport	Freq.	Angle
Football	8	120
Baseball	4	60
Tennis	1	
Basketball	5	
Hockey	2	30
Swimming	4	60

14. What is the angle for Basketball?

15. Six people join the youth club. They choose Football, Football, Basketball, Swimming, Swimming and Baseball. What is the new angle for swimming?

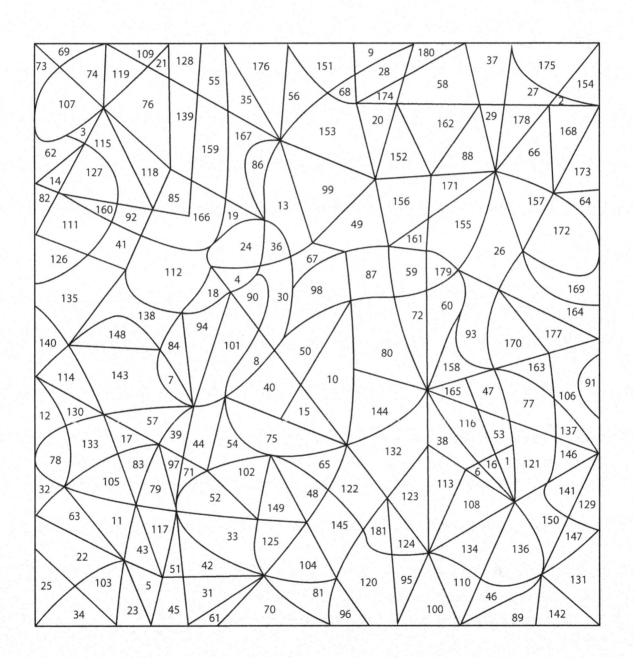

8

HISTOGRAMS

PART 1: 1. 2. 3. 4. 5. Calculate the frequency density for each group.

CHALLENGE:
Draw the histogram.

Test score	Frequency	Frequency density
$0 \leq s < 30$	33	
$30 \leq s < 50$	35	
$50 \leq s < 70$	41	
$70 \leq s < 80$	39	
$80 \leq s < 100$	32	

PART 2: The histogram and the table show the daily temperature in degrees Celsius.

6, 7, 8, 9, 10. Complete the table.

Temperature	Frequency	Frequency density
$0 \leq t < 6$		1
$6 \leq t < 10$	8	
$10 \leq t < 12$		3.5
$12 \leq t < 16$	6	
$16 \leq t < 24$		1

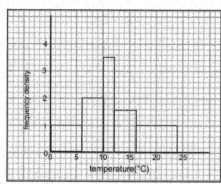

PART 3: Here is an incomplete histogram.
Use the fact that there are 10 people represented by the bar for $130 \leq h < 135$ to work out the scale for the frequency density axis.

11. How many people are between $110 \leq h < 120$cm tall?
12. What is the frequency density for $125 \leq h < 130$?
13. There are 6 people in the $135 \leq h < 150$ category. What is the frequency density?
14. What percentage are over 130cm tall?
15. How many people are less than 126cm tall?

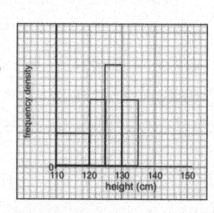

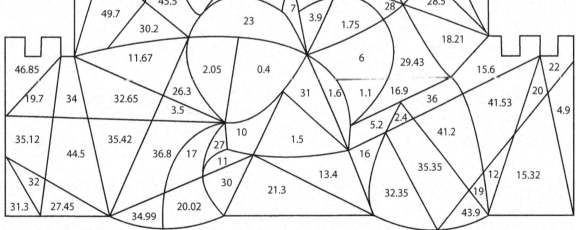

CUMULATIVE FREQUENCY

PART 1: The frequency table shows information about the times taken to complete a crossword puzzle by 100 people.

1. How many people took between 15 and 20 minutes?
2. Complete the cumulative frequency for $10 \le t < 20$.
3. Complete the cumulative frequency for $10 \le t < 30$.
4. How many people completed the puzzle in less than 25 minutes?
5. How many people took longer than 25 minutes?

Time	Frequency	Cumulative Frequency
$10 \le t < 15$	16	16
$15 \le t < 20$	22	
$20 \le t < 25$	45	83
$25 \le t < 30$	10	
$30 \le t < 35$	7	100

PART 2: The cumulative frequency graph show the marks gained in a Geography test.

6. Use the graph to find the cumulative frequency for $0 \le m < 40$.
7. Use the graph to find the cumulative frequency for $0 \le m < 80$.
8. How many students achieved a score of at least 40?
9. Estimate the median score.
10. The teacher wants less than 10 people to fail. What should the pass score be?

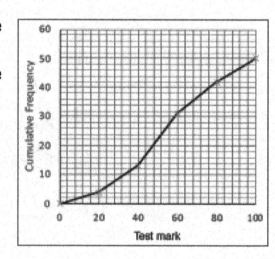

PART 3: The table shows the number of hours spent revising for a test.

11, 12. Complete the table.

13. Draw the cumulative frequency curve and use it to estimate the median.

14. How many people spent less than 3 hours revising?

15. How many people spent more than 9 hour revising?

Time	Frequency	Cumulative Frequency
$0 \le h < 2$	20	20
$2 \le h < 4$	25	
$4 \le h < 6$	28	73
$6 \le h < 8$	10	83
$8 \le h < 10$	7	

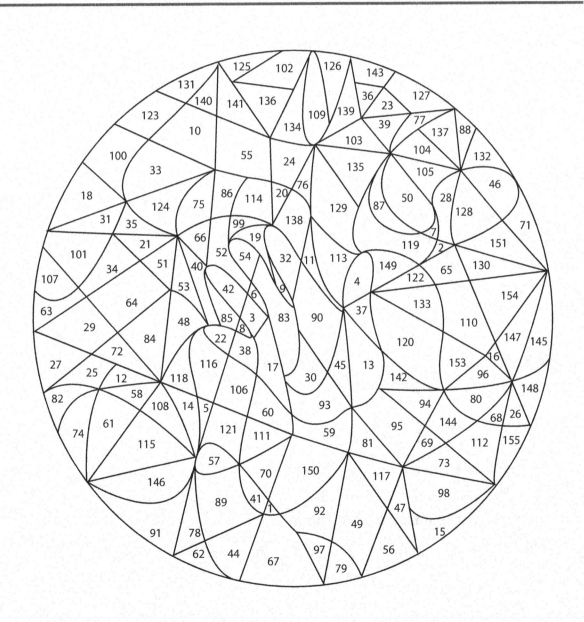

10

BOX AND WHISKER PLOTS AND QUARTILES

PART 1: Here is a set of data.

8 15 15 22 35 14 10 13 29 24 14 18 17 19 21

Work out:

1. The minimum
2. The lower quartile
3. The median
4. The upper quartile
5. The maximum

PART 2: Here is a box and whisker plot.

6. What was the median score?
7. What was the highest score?
8. What was the lower quartile?
9. What is the interquartile range?
10. What percentage scored lower than 35?

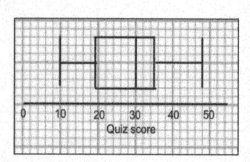

PART 3: The ages of people going to see three different movies at a theatre were recorded and displayed as box plots.

11. What was the age of the youngest person asked?
12. What was the median age of the people that went to see movie C?
13. What was the interquartile range for movie C?

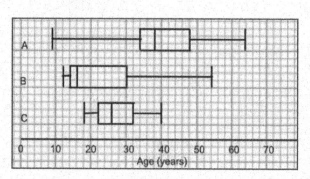

14. What is the range of the ages for movie A?

15. Movie B was preferred by high school students. What percentage were less than 16 years old?

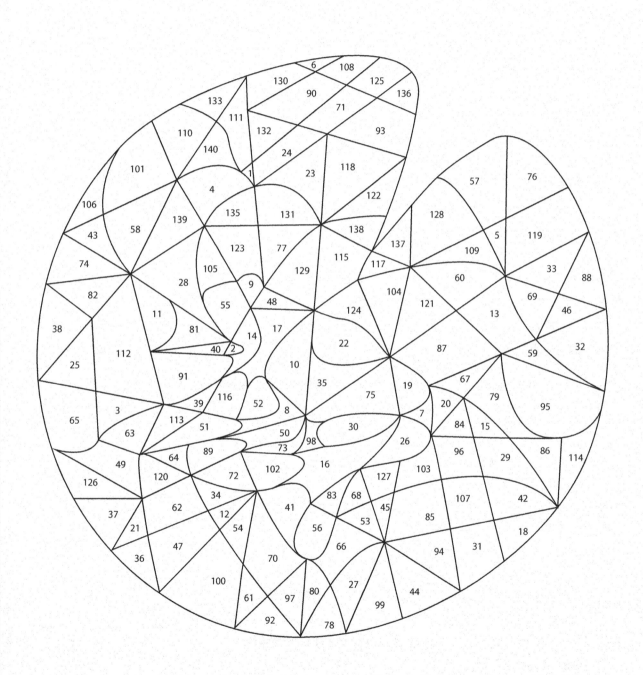

VENN DIAGRAMS

PART 1: The Venn diagram shows the number of students that play football, hockey and rugby.

How many students:

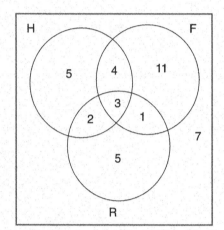

1. Are in the class?
2. Do not play football or hockey or rugby?
3. Play hockey?
4. Play football and hockey but not rugby?
5. Play football, hockey and rugby?

PART 2: 32 teenagers go to 3 different clubs organised by the school. Everyone goes to at least one club. 6 only go to art. 5 go to all 3 clubs. 2 go to chess and art. 15 go to art. 3 only go to chess and 6 only go to dance.

Draw the Venn diagram to show this information. How many teenagers:

6. Go to chess and dance but not art?
7. Go to chess?
8. Go to dance?
9. Go to one club only?
10. Go to at least 2 clubs

PART 3: The Venn diagram shows the number of cars in a car park.

11. Calculate the value of x.
12. How many red cars were recorded?
13. How many cars were either red, Japanese or both?
14. How many Japanese cars that were not red were there?
15. A car is chosen at random. What is the probability (as a percentage) that it is red?

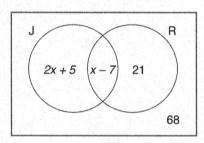

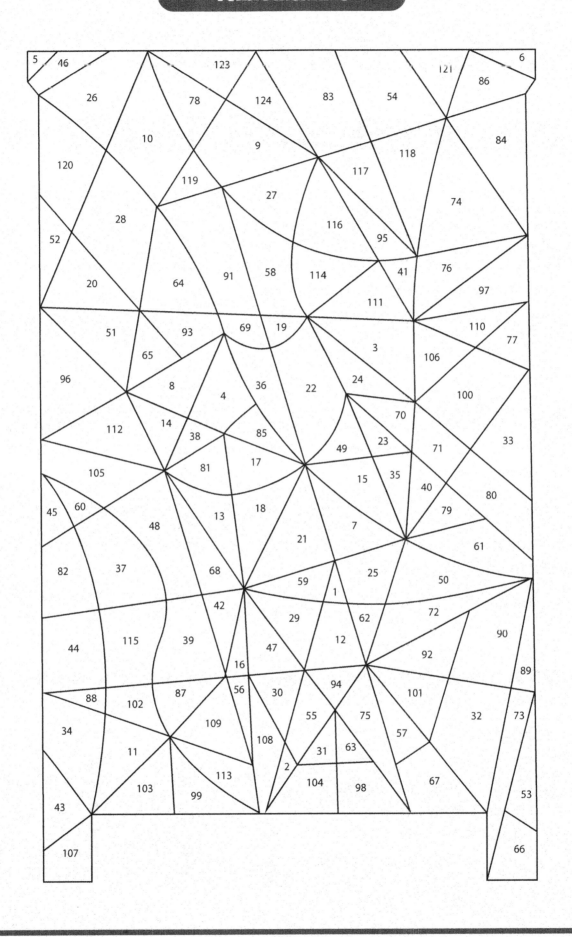

PROBABILITY 1

(basic, including sample space diagrams)

PART 1: Look at the word PROBABILITY. A letter is chosen at random. What is the probability that it is:

1. An A?
2. A vowel?
3. A B?

4. In the word TAIL?
5. Not an R?

PART 2: A bag contains 4 red counters, 5 blue counters and 6 green counters. One counter is chosen at random. What is the probability that it is:

6. Red?   7. Red or green?   8. White?

A green counter is removed. One counter is chosen at random. What is the probability that it is:

9. Green?
10. Red?

PART 3: Two dice are rolled at random and the total recorded. The sample space diagram shows the possible totals. What is:

11. P(total = 12)?
12. P(total = 4)?
13. P(total is a square number)?
14. P(total is ≤5)?
15. P(total is 7 or 8)?

+	1	2	3	4	5	6
1	2	3	4	5	6	7
2	3	4	5	6	7	8
3	4	5	6	7	8	9
4	5	6	7	8	9	10
5	6	7	8	9	10	11
6	7	8	9	10	11	12

Give each answer as a fraction in its lowest terms.

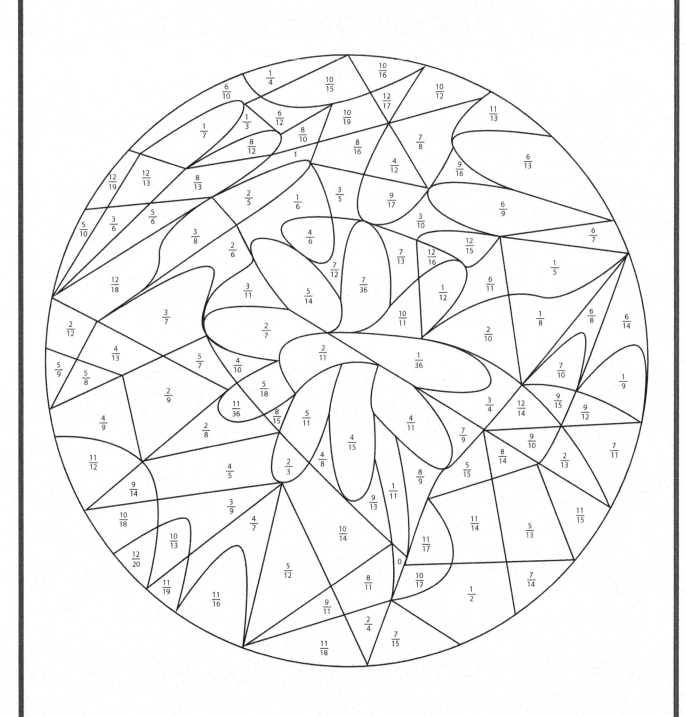

PROBABILITY 2

(tree diagrams, with replacement)

PART 1: Kathy and Dave play two games, game A and game B. The probability that Kathy wins game A is 0.6. The probability Kathy wins game B is 0.3. There are no draws. Draw a tree diagram.

1. Calculate P (Kathy loses game A)
2. Calculate P (Dave wins game B)
3. Calculate P (Kathy wins both)
4. Calculate P (Dave wins game A then Kathy wins game B)
5. Calculate P (Dave wins at least one game)

PART 2: There are 8 blue counters and 2 red counters in a bag. A counter is chosen at random, its color noted and then returned to the bag. A second counter is then selected at random and its color noted. Calculate:

6. P (blue counter)
7. P (red counter)
8. P (two blue counters are chosen)
9. P (both counters are the same color)
10. P (blue counter then red counter)

PART 3: Scarlett does a crossword and a Sudoku every day. The probability of Scarlett completing the Sudoku is 0.9. The probability of Scarlett completing both is 0.72. Calculate:

11. P (not completing the Sudoku)
12. P (not completing either of them)
13. P (completing just one of them)
14. P (completing at least one of them)

Give all answers as a decimal.

15. During September Scarlett does the crossword every day and completes 28 of them. If the probability of Scarlett completing the Sudoku stays the same, what is P (completing both) now?

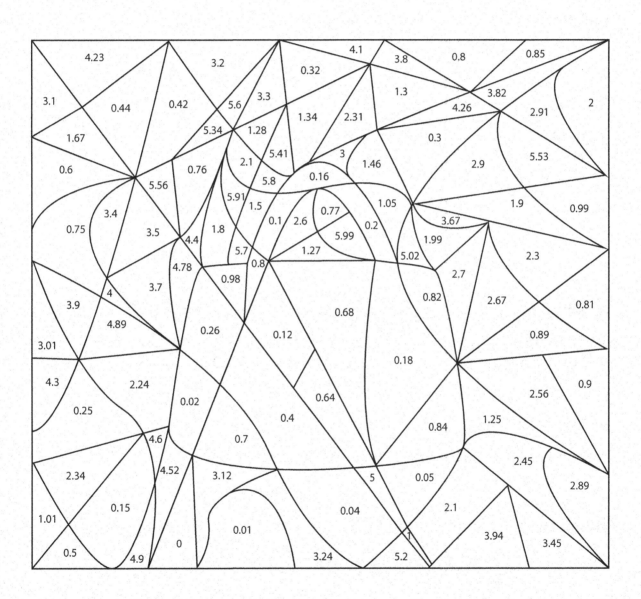

PROBABILITY 3

(expectation)

PART 1: Douglas rolls one fair six-sided dice 300 times.

1.   How many 6's does he expect to get?
2.   How often does he expect it to land on an even number?
3.   How often does he expect to see it land on 1 or 2?

Jack flips a coin 20 times.

4.   How many tails does Jack expect to see?

Jack actually gets 6 tails so he thinks the coin might be biased. To test this he flips the coin 100 times.

5.   If he is correct, how many tails does he expect to see?

PART 2: There are some counters in a bag. The probability of choosing a red or green counter is shown in the table. There are twice as many red counters as blue ones. The remaining counters are yellow.

Calculate the remaining probabilities first.

Color	Red	Yellow	Blue	Green
Probability	0.4			0.3

If there are 60 counters in the bag, how many are:

6. Red   7. Yellow   8. Blue   9. Green

When they are counted there are actually 80 counters in the bag.

10.   How many more red counters are there than was originally expected?

PART 3: Jane plants 40 seeds and 32 produce healthy plants.

11.   What percentage of the seeds produced a plant?
12.   Jane planted another 120 seeds. How many plants does she expect to see?

In the summer the plants produce flowers. The original 32 plants gave 16 red flowers, 4 pink flowers and 12 white flowers. Of the next 120 plants

13. How many will have red flowers?
14. How many will have pink flowers?
15. How many will have white flowers?

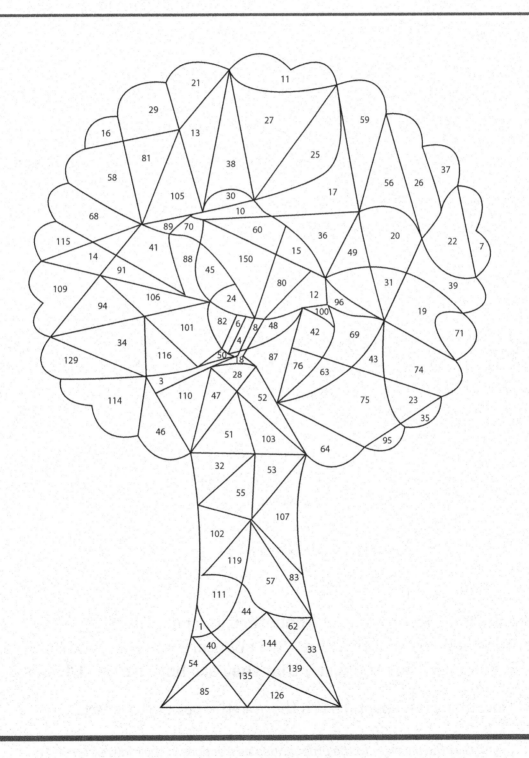

PROBABILITY 4

(tree diagrams, without replacement)

PART 1: After my birthday I have a bag of candy left. There are 5 chocolates and 4 toffees left. I choose one at random from the bag and eat it. I then choose a second candy and eat that.

1. Given that the first candy I ate was a chocolate, what is the probability that the second candy is a chocolate?
2. Given that the first candy I ate was a toffee, what is the probability that the second candy is a toffee?
3. Calculate P (I eat 2 chocolates)
4. Calculate P (I eat 1 chocolate and 1 toffee)
5. Calculate P (I eat no chocolates)

PART 2: Charlie has 5 black socks, 3 white socks and 2 red socks in a drawer. He likes to pick two socks at random with his eyes closed to see if he has a pair. He picks one sock, puts it to one side and then picks a second sock.

6. Given that the first sock he picked was a black sock, what is the probability that the second sock is black too?
7. Calculate P (both socks are black)
8. Calculate P (both socks are the same color)
9. Calculate P (at least one sock is white)
10. Calculate P (he chooses a white sock followed by a red sock)

PART 3: There is a total of 21 counters in a pot. There are n red counters and the rest are blue. Two counters are removed from the pot at random. The probability that they are both red is 0.1. Calculate:

11. How many red counters are there in the pot at the start?

Give the answers to the probabilities as fractions in their lowest terms.

12. Given that the first counter was red, what is the probability that the second counter is also red?

13. Given that the first counter was blue, what is the probability that the second counter is red?

14. What is the probability of picking a red counter followed by a blue counter?

15. What is the probability that the two counters are both blue?

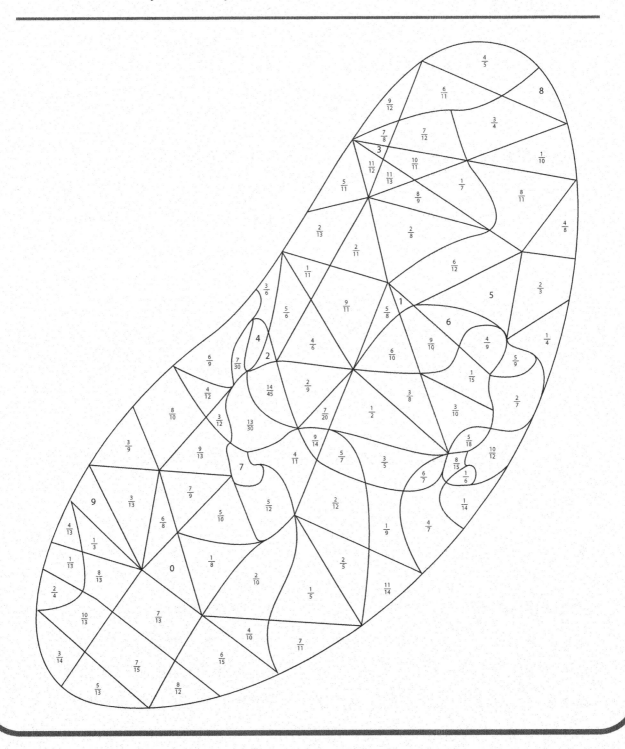

answers

1. DIAGRAMS

Part 1: 20, 9, 3, 63, 42

Part 2: 4, 13, 25, 48, 50

Part 3: 90, 40, 24, 52, 60

2. AVERAGES 1

Part 1: 7, 17, 45, 1, 4

Part 2: 70, 24, 14, 23, 3

Part 3: 12, 31, 94, 6, 11

3. AVERAGES 2

Part 1: 6, 22, 20, 453, 23

Part 2: 17, 25, 80, 1050, 13

Part 3: 5, 200, 4, 300, 75

4. MEAN, MEDIAN, MODE AND RANGE

Part 1: 4, 7.3, 27, 17, 34

Part 2: 35, 32, 31.4, 15, 5

Part 3: 9, 20, 200, 28, 22.9

5. CORRELATION

Part 1: 10, 11, 7, 5, 9

Part 2: 20, 95, 70, 85, 45

Part 3: 1200, 850, 15, 1300, 1050

6. FREQUENCY POLYGONS

Part 1: 14, 1, 20, 100, 1.6

Part 2: 10, 44, 36, 2, 2.4

Part 3: 18, 60, 26, 97, 55

7. PIE CHARTS

Part 1: 36, 10, 40, 80, 30

Part 2: 144, 4, 18, 8, 60

Part 3: 24, 50, 15, 75, 72

8. HISTOGRAMS

Part 1: 1.1, 1.75, 2.05, 3.9, 1.6

Part 2: 6, 2, 7, 1.5, 8

Part 3: 10, 3, 0.4, 31, 23

9. CUMULATIVE FREQUENCY

Part 1: 22, 38, 93, 83, 17

Part 2: 13, 42, 37, 54, 32

Part 3: 45, 90, 4, 30, 3

10. BOX PLOTS

Part 1: 8, 14, 17, 22, 35

Part 2: 30, 48, 19, 16, 75

Part 3: 9, 26, 10, 55, 50

Answers

11. VENN DIAGRAMS

Part 1: 38, 7, 14, 4, 3

Part 2: 8, 18, 21, 15, 17

Part 3: 22, 36, 85, 49, 24

12. PROBABILITY 1

Part 1: 1/11, 4/11, 2/11, 5/11, 10/11

Part 2: 4/15, 2/3, 0, 5/14, 2/7

Part 3: 1/36, 1/12, 7/36, 5/18, 11/36

13. PROBABILITY 2

Part 1: 0.4, 0.7, 0.18, 0.12, 0.82

Part 2: 0.8, 0.2, 0.64, 0.68, 0.16

Part 3: 0.1 0.02, 0.26, 0.98, 0.84

14. PROBABILITY 3

Part 1: 50, 150, 100, 10, 30

Part 2: 24, 6, 12, 18, 8

Part 3: 80, 96, 60, 15, 45

15. PROBABILITY 4

Part 1: 1/2, 3/8, 5/18, 5/9, 1/6

Part 2: 4/9, 2/9, 14/45, 8/15, 1/15

Part 3: 7, 3/10, 7/20, 7/30, 13/30

SOLVED PUZZLES

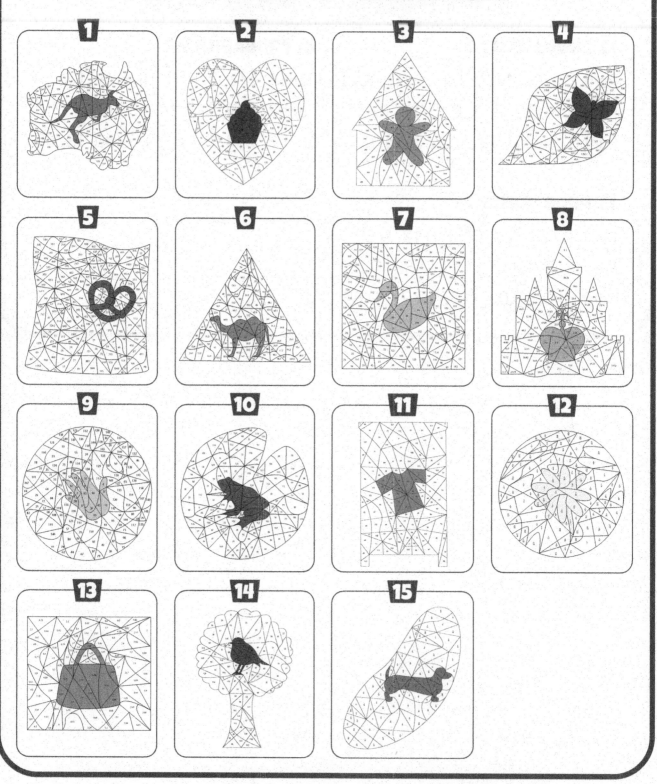